Country Cats City People

Country Cats City People

~

Breaking the Myth about Feline Ferals inside Tuxedo Park

SHEILA POMPAN

EDITOR ~ LAURA SHAINE CUNNINGHAM

ISBN-10: 1505381754
ISBN-13: 9781505381757
Library of Congress Control Number: 2015900895
CreateSpace Independent Publishing Platform
North Charleston, South Carolina

DEDICATION

As I always have and will continue to do, I dedicate my books to you.
To my husband, Gerard (Gary) Pompan.

TABLE OF CONTENTS

ACKNOWLEDGMENTS

First and foremost to my husband Gary, who always believed this story was worth telling and who rallied my enthusiasm when I became discouraged. I am grateful to Hilda Morales who I can always depend on and who continues to care for our cat family when we are away. She has been with me on this journey of feline magic from the very beginning. To all of my writing teachers and colleagues whose tireless encouragement and feedback to keep writing continues to inspire and motivate me to pick up the pen, trust, be brave and write my truth. Particularly the Progoff Intensive Journal Program and the Memoir Institute.

My dear friend and fellow feline care giver Jennifer Gillooley who provided insight and honesty during many editorial stages. Thank you. My Tuxedo Park neighbors, who first introduced me to their own "wild feral cats" all those years ago, Jim and Nancy Hays, ChuYin and Gardner Hempel and Carolyn Roberts. Your guidance, laughter and love of your own feline families encouraged this story. To Deborah Larkin and Heidi Hamilton, whose beautiful gardens continue to fuel my writing as well as providing delightful play for our outdoor feline friends. Always dependable for honest feedback and editorial comments, avid readers Rita Perrault and Robin Randolph. To Heather Keltz who came in at the final hour with her invaluable expertise. I thank you!

Abiding thanks to Joni Mantell LCSW, CSW whose expertise in adoption and infertility encouraged me to dig deeper into the truths behind this story.

Christian Sonne, Tuxedo Park Historian has given his time graciously, shared a wealth of historical information and whose confirmation of facts and events have assisted in providing accuracy to this story.

And to my feline family. You have opened up feelings inside of Gary and I that had been closed off entirely or that had never been felt before. You have taught us you can never be kind enough, that compassion, patience and trust grow in steps and that love is abundant. Whether giving or receiving, these traits are a universal language understood by all species.

During the early beginnings of writing this story, I called on the expertise of an author whose ease of writing words I continue to aspire to. Now my editor on this book, Laura Shaine Cunningham's wisdom, expertise and laughter has inspired, motivated and pushed me to think, create, trust and write with all the passion of my being and beyond. Finally to all the felines that have bridged me with my fellow humans over the years, I am grateful.

A place in the country is where we will be
Where cats and kittens and nature roam free
Heavy the rhythms of cicadas at night
The moon and the stars shine sparkling bright.
Lessons are learned from our animal friends.
If only we'd listen
No need to pretend.
8/25/2014

INTRODUCTION

If we hadn't found the Country Place, we would never have met the Country Cats…We thought we were buying only a house….We didn't know that we had entered another world, and would find a Cat Family who would fully awaken longing needs and desires that had lain dormant for so long.

It's often said we don't choose our family we choose our friends. But can a family be created? Yes it can. A family, in the conventional sense, can provide you with shelter, protection, support and a myriad of definitions. What if we were to look outside those traditional definitions that we've been taught? What if we accepted those feelings that may in fact be natural to us, but not typical, should we break that traditional lineage? What if we didn't have any other choice? Recognizing those natural instincts is the first step, looking towards another direction is the next.

It's not for the faint of heart to be on the road less travelled. Its path is unknown, often unfamiliar and even frightening at times. Yet, if we take that chance and walk its course, the results can be even more fulfilling than you ever imagined. I have learned that so many of the natural gifts we have been given, that surround us, can provide an abundance of fulfillment and joy that we might have otherwise not known, had we not been able to recognize them. More often than not, they come in the most unexpected ways and in the most unlikely places.

CITY PEOPLE

The Village of Tuxedo Park, NY is located 38 miles North of the big Island called Manhattan also known as N.Y.C. There are more people who haven't heard of Tuxedo Park than have. Even for those people like me who grew up in the great Empire State. It was by chance that my husband and I found the Village of Tuxedo Park. We noticed a real estate ad in the *Wall Street Journal* when print was still fashionable and the primary mode of news. The ad read, "Just 45 minutes from NY." We took a drive over the George Washington Bridge to the Palisades Parkway where life instantly changed from the hectic turn top of city life to green grass, views of the Hudson River and lots of sunshine.

Fresh air at last! 'We should get out of the city more often,' we thought to ourselves. We turned off exit 9W to the NYS thruway. After a few exits we saw our exit, 15B. We got off and made a left on 17 North to the town.

Our contact from the ad was the owner of Tuxedo Park Estates, an affiliate of Christies at the time. She gave us perfect directions, "Our office is across from the post office," when you pass the Orange Top diner, get in the left lane and pull into Tuxedo Square. If you go to the blinking light you've gone too far," she said.

We found her office easily enough, and after making the proper introductions, our house hunt began. It all felt so mysterious, so exciting. Our realtor drove us through these massive stone gates which provided the entrance to the Park and narrow winding roads. At that time of season trees in their dormancy lined the roads and the sky covered the Village with the most brilliant hues of blue. The Park with its winding roads, narrow from their origin in horse-and-carriage days, had a mysterious, gilded charm left over from its original era.

We saw the three lakes, which are beautiful, and a private country club that is situated perfectly towards the sun. At one point in time even an ice skating rink was offered that was available for winter activities. One of the few and rare court tennis facilities in the country remains here, and serves as host to the club's annual Gold Racquets tournament, typically held during the month of February. Left on our own accord, it was easy to become lost in the maze of narrow winding roads.

Which is exactly what happened. Maps of the Village were sacredly guarded at that time, in large part because of the high profile residents—both past and present, Caryn Johnson (aka Whoopi Goldberg), Robert Duvall, Cyndi Lauper, basketball players and corporate executives have owned property in Tuxedo Park. Privacy is a highly respected value amongst Tuxedo Park residents and the reason so many luminaries moved here.

I remember exploring the winding hills and narrow roads, but I most distinctly recall driving on a road that went up a steep hill to a point where you could see the largest lake, Tuxedo Lake. The road led to a driveway of what I still consider to be one of the most magnificent homes in the Park, a large mansion that at the time was painted yellow and was said to be owned by an NBA player. As we reached a dead end we realized this road became a driveway and that we may have been on private property. Aware of the diligence of the Village Police, we quickly tried to turn around which took a few tries of backing up, putting it in drive, putting it in reverse, turning the wheel, moving forward. Finally we got the car turned around and drove fast down the hill admiring the views and laughing hysterically, and while looking at each other both said at the same time "we are going to live here." We were smitten by the magical beauty that surrounded us, combined with such a short and easy commute to Manhattan, where we could split our time between the city and country.

It was Pierre Lorillard IV heir to the largest tobacco company in the U.S. and Bruce Price the American architect and father of the *Etiquette* author Emily

Post who created Tuxedo Park in 1885. The property was originally owned by Lorillard's great grandfather purchased in 1814. For many years the Lorillard family used the land to cut lumber and occasionally hunted and fished. Pierre Lorillard IV sold his summer estate in Newport and developed the 13,000 acres in Tuxedo which he had inherited from his great grandfather and this he decided would be the perfect location to create his weekend fishing and hunting reserve yet still be close enough to New York City. He purchased several acres of land, and hired Bruce Price as architect to build the first of several mansions and cottages for his family and other wealthy associates to summer in, along with homes for the chauffeurs and stables for the horses.

After looking at a few homes, we settled on one. A historic carriage house once owned by the first wife of the very famous Alfred Lee Loomis. Alfred Lee Loomis the Wall Street tycoon as he is often referred to was a scientist, a lawyer and a master mathematician.

While practicing law, Loomis was fascinated with physics and all things scientific. He kept a secret laboratory in Tuxedo Park where he experimented with supersonic sound waves and radar, eventually assisting the government with the development of radar within the army and the development of the atomic bomb, later known as the Manhattan Project during World War II. Loomis was a brilliant mind whose dozens of new projects and innovations changed the course of science, physics and history.

Loomis married twice. His first wife was Ellen H. Farnsworth who bore him three children. His second wife was Manette Seeldrayers Hobart. While still married to Ellen, he was having a secret affair with Manette. Manette was the wife of his best friend and assistant in several of his early experiments. Manette and Alfred carried on their affairs in a home known as the Glass House. Loomis built this house on several acres of land just below The Tower House, which would eventually become his primary laboratory. The Glass House was an early solar home that included air conditioning and electricity and considered quite advanced for this period. Eventually he divorced Ellen, leaving her in their home on Club House Rd., now known as Fox Hill Rd. In 1926 Loomis purchased another home in Tuxedo Park, the Spencer Trask house on Crows Nest Rd. This home was also referred to as The Tower House. Deep within the confines of its basement would be his infamous laboratory. Throughout the 1920's until 1940 Loomis conducted numerous experiments in Tuxedo Park, setting up laboratories in each and every home where he lived. In one such house, just down the hill from his home on Club House Rd., and the one we purchased, his very early experiments with super sonic sound waves were performed.

Ellen Farnsworth Loomis initially appeared to be a good match for Alfred. Originally from Boston and daughter of a prominent New England family, she was highly educated in languages and the arts, perhaps making her more tolerable than the average woman of her time with her husband's obsessions in scientific experimentations. Often he used her as a subject in his experiments which some say was not such a good thing for Ellen. Ellen suffered from depression throughout her life. This seems partly due to the isolation she experienced as a result of Alfred's obsessions and absence from home. It could also have been a result of her brother's death. Very early in their marriage Ellen's brother died in War I and some say she was never able to fully recover. She was hospitalized for her illness several times. On one occasion, Alfred had her doctor prescribe orders that prevented her children and any visitors from seeing her while she was institutionalized. She felt abandoned which only worsened her depression. During this period Alfred also wanted a divorce so that he could marry Manette. When his sons learned about the affair strained relations continued for the rest of their lives. In those days when divorce was highly unusual and frowned upon in society. Alfred fell out of social circles both in Tuxedo Park and New York Society as a result of his hidden affair and eventual marriage to Manette.

Socially Ellen never enjoyed the many gatherings at the Tuxedo Club. She did serve on the board of Trustees of the Tuxedo Park Library from 1919 until 1940. She was very fond of children and was often spotted reading to them at the library. She was also fond of animals and cared for several felines while living in her home on Club House Road. Ellen was beautiful and charming and was able to fundraise on a significant scale for the library, although not every event was successful. I heard one story about Ellen that could be true today as well as then. On one occasion she invited a prominent author to speak at a fund raiser for the Tuxedo Library one Spring. After much coaxing the author finally agreed to do it. At the event hardly anyone showed up. Mrs. Loomis said, "The people from the Hamlet thought it was for people from the Park, and the people from the Park thought it was for people from the Hamlet."

Ellen Farnsworth Loomis left her mark on Tuxedo Park. I always felt a keen sense of pride owning the carriage house that once belonged to her. Viewing the survey of our home with her name on the deed brings a smile to my face to this day. Ellen passed away in November 1975 at the age of 85. Her ashes are buried on the grounds of St. Mary's Episcopal church here in Tuxedo Park.

Across the street from our home was once The Racetrack. Lorillard envisioned his retreat with not only the Clubhouse, tennis house and grounds for fishing and hunting but it also was to include harness racing and horse shows. There was a wooden grandstand installed at the southeast area of the track. Box seats were reserved for subscribed members or by those from outside of Tuxedo who were closely connected to club members. Women arrived dressed immaculately in the fashion of the day and men wore blazers complete with straw or bowler hats. There are many photos of the Racetrack at the Tuxedo Historical Society located on Hospital Rd. in the town of Tuxedo New York. I've walked the racetrack several times. You can still see its circular shape imbedded in the grounds. Today it's home to several species of butterflies, plants and birds. I never tire viewing the old racetrack from our house up on the hill, particularly during the winter months when it is glistening from the snow and wrapped in blue from the sky overhead, while the sun shimmers its rays creating a bowl of sparking jewels.

RESIDENTS

O ur initiation as newbies consisted of soirees, galas and social events. There were Historical Society parties, election parties, events surrounding the country and golf club, events linked to the church and cocktail parties for no other reason than to gather and catch up with fellow "Parkies," a term that distinguishes those who live inside the Village behind the gates from those that reside in the Hamlet, which is part of the town of Tuxedo owned and originally built by Lorillard. As with all parties, gossip and story telling abound. We learned about the famous architects Bruce Price, Warren and Wetmore, and James Brown Lord who built several of the historic mansions. The unparalleled skill of the Italian laborers, craftsmen and masons who built stone walls, bridal paths and the stone foundations supporting the numerous mansions throughout the Park, is nearly impossible to match today. Although many of the original grand mansions are now gone, due partly from neglect or fires to collect insurance during the Great Depression, there still remains a significant number of these homes today. When I'm cruising on my eighteen foot electric boat, the only type of boats allowed on our Lakes due to the fact that the Tuxedo Lake is also the source of our drinking water, I'm reminded of romantic Lago Como in Italy.

Men in top hats and tails getting off the train to their sportmen's retreat. Women opening up their country homes for the season with help from their servants threaded with all of the historical data, stories and tales. Legend or fact? Most likely a mixture of both. For me, my favorite story has long been about how and where the tuxedo suit got its name. At the 2011 annual Autumn Ball for the Tuxedo Historical Society held at the Tuxedo Club, the credit for discovery of this sporty dinner jacket was once again up for debate. The story I had been told previously gave credit to Griswold Lorillard, who was the youngest son of tobacco magnate and original Tuxedo Park founder Pierre Lorillard IV. It's been said Pierre's son Griswold pulled a stunt at the first Autumn Ball in 1886. After being frustrated with his tails interfering with dancing and sitting, he emerged at the ball having cut off his tails from his dress coat, thus creating the tuxedo. The version from the 2011 Autumn Ball gave credit elsewhere. According to a representative of Henry Poole and Company, a gentlemen's tailor from London, Henry Poole made a short evening smoking jacket for the Prince of Whales to wear at an informal dinner party. In 1886, James Potter, a resident of Tuxedo Park was invited to join the Prince of Wales at his country estate in Sandringham. While there, he too had a smoking jacket made by the Prince's tailors Henry Poole and Co. When James returned to Tuxedo Park he proudly showed off his new dinner jacket at the Tuxedo Club. According to Christian Sonne Tuxedo Park Historian, legend has it that many gentlemen wore the more compatible and informal dinner jacket in Tuxedo Park, and when their friends in the city took up the more comfortable dinner jacket they named it a tuxedo. Perhaps our feline friends gamboled the tale of this story with one of their own, behind the gates of Tuxedo Park!

O nce we purchased the house, we were given permission to enter the Park. Now we could feel the mystique of the Village by driving through it on our own, which is an adventure in and of itself. Generally, you have to be a resident in order to enter Tuxedo Park. We even have specific tags that attach to the front of our license plates to distinguish residents from non residents. These tags are labeled with the letter R indicating resident status and NR indicating non resident status. Non residents may be the parents who pick up their children from the Tuxedo Park School, contractors, nannies or Members of the Tuxedo Club. The entrance gate is patrolled by a police guard. When you pull up to the gate, if you have a tag the police will let you through, but if you do not, the police will ask you what is your purpose in entering. If you're not visiting a resident, or have any other non-resident business in the park, then you can be turned away.

In May of 2001, we finally moved into our first country home, originally intended for weekend getaways. On September 11, 2001 that changed. Like so many Americans, life as we knew it had radically altered and would never be the same. I had been working for a major insurance company as VP of Human Resources. We had two locations where I worked, mid-town and Tower One of the World Trade Center. Like so many Americans at that time, we made life-changing decisions after September 11th and as a couple we decided we would be spending much more of our time at our country home.

After years of travelling, career building and living in the concrete jungle where professional dreams can be fulfilled, the country setting introduced us to new discoveries. I thought I had seen nature but realized I had never really experienced it the way I believe that I was meant to— to see deer running free, twin fawns and their doe, black bear with cubs that climbed in our tree, woodchucks, yellow birds, blue birds, cardinals, butterflies in yellow, black, orange and blue. And, every once in awhile, on that rare but exciting occasion, I would spot a cat, those magnificent, beautiful feline creatures which I've always chosen as my pets ever since I was a child.

Several years went by of establishing my gardens, initially by myself and then after several bouts of poison ivy, with the expertise of Deborah Larkin, owner of Sundance Gardens, a professional landscaping company. I learned to create a home that would be a respite from the chaos of this new world. Our country was now at war, but here in Tuxedo Park, nature was still in balance. Nature worked magnificently from sunrise to sunset, from dusk to dawn. There was an orchestrated dance which nature choreographed in perfect harmony. Fireflies put on a brilliant show at dusk, followed by nocturnal stirrings, the sounds of cicadas orchestrated with a precision that could be transcribed by most any composer.

When the sun rose, birds of all sizes and species began to sing their chorus. So many tones to listen to! I could watch the daily activities of the chipmunks and squirrels, always busy doing what they do—chasing one another, scouting nuts and storing them. Changing seasons brought changing scenes with majestic images and intoxicating smells. Each fall brought anticipation of brilliant hues of color, blowing leaves that fell and luxuriated the ground with enchanting candy colors. Pine cones drop and are then collected to jump start the warmth that oak and birch logs bring when they burn in a fireplace. During the winter months the Park expands, appearing larger and more grand with the fall of glistening white flakes and blankets of fresh white virgin snow. Lights from inside cozy homes cast an orange effervescent glow creating a whimsical feeling throughout the entire Park. You can almost feel the many lives that have passed through these gates, including Loomis himself, when the quiet settles during this time of year. This was a welcome respite from my city life. My curiosity peaked and my communion with nature truly began.

Tuxedo Park Cats

It was here where new interactions began with the species with which I have felt most strongly drawn to--Those beautiful mysterious felines, better known as the domestic cat. This country environment was much different from the suburbs where I grew up. There, cats sat on windowsills and observed their predators, which were primarily neighborhood dogs, from the safety of their cozy, warm abodes. If allowed to venture outside, everyone knew which cat belonged to whom and the cats knew which neighbors would be feline friendly and where they wouldn't be welcomed. But in Tuxedo Park, behind the gates, life couldn't be more different for my feline friends who lived entirely outdoors. More dangerous predators lurked from every direction, from up above, from behind, and around every corner. Hawks, fox, raccoons, coyotes, and even other cats marked their territory making life for my feline friends very difficult. It is a twenty-four hour job just to survive, making those quick cat naps nearly impossible.

THE FERALS, THE STRAYS .....
WHAT'S IN A NAME?

Where I live, there are what folks around here call "feral cats." Although I've been a cat owner most of my life, I had never heard of feral cats. Where I grew up, my family had indoor/outdoor cats that roamed around during the day, took evening walks with our collie dog, watched our home from high up in our lone tree in the front yard and scratched on our door to be let inside when they wanted to eat, then sleep in our cozy beds with us when it was bedtime. But here there was a different breed of cat. After all, my curiosity and hunger to take care of something or someone was a perfect match for these roaming feral cats, and as the stars would align, for one cat in particular.

What are they? Who are they? I had been warned by a few neighbors in Tuxedo Park, that the feral cats here were wild, untrainable and have feline leukemia. They had even more cautionary remarks:

"You're never going to get them near you."

"If you see one prowling around, be afraid, be very afraid"! *Hmm,* this to me only raised my curiosity and became a challenge and mystery that I had to resolve and unfold.

As I got to know my neighbors, I observed that some of them too were lovers of cats. 'Great,' I thought, I can fulfill my void from the loss of Miko, a calico cat who was my companion for almost 20 years, with visits to my neighbors' cats. One, by one, I would ask them about their cute cats.

"Where did you get them?"

"Don't tell anyone," they would say, "but he just kept coming around and I felt so bad for the cat so we bought him an igloo, you know, those very large plastic homes that you can purchase at your local pet store."

"Oh," I said, "I never heard of those, why don't you just let them indoors?"

"The igloo is for their protection from the outside elements. We don't allow them to come inside... well we do, when we feed them."

"Oh" I said, "Aren't you afraid they'll destroy everything, being wild?"

No answer. Silence. On another occasion, I noticed a small laundry room while visiting my neighbor; the room was off the kitchen and I saw that there were two bowls next to each other and neatly placed on top of kitty placemats. *Hmmm...* cat bowls, I suspected because of their small size. To the left corner of the room was a tidy box, another name for a litter box. The secret was revealed. A wild cat has been domesticated and found its rightful owner to train, thereby providing his every feline indulgence!

On a visit to another neighbor's home, we met a cat named Bun. Bun is shy and quiet and looks very much like the other neighbors' cats. In fact, all these cats in Tuxedo Park have surprisingly very similar traits and markings. Black or grey bodies, white vests, white spats and black or grey tails... *tuxedo* cats living inside the Village of *Tuxedo* Park? Mysterious coincidence? I wonder. *Hmmm...* more on that later.

Bun never comes when the owner calls and runs away when people visit. Hmmm, I say to my neighbor, "how long have you had Bun?"

"Oh a couple of years."

"Do you bring him back and forth from the city?"

"No, Well sometimes," my neighbor says. I sense she too, like the others had been reluctant to divulge too much. I learned that Bun has a girlfriend who sits outside and peers in at Bun thru sliding glass doors. After several months and a very cold winter, I learn that Bun's girlfriend has now been adopted and moved indoors, keeping Bun warm and living with him as his new companion!

My curiosity was rising higher regarding the feral cats and I wished that they would come to my house. I began to wonder how I could attract them to my home?

My first thought was --why not grow catnip? I can't remember if it was the catnip or the cat that came around first, but what I do recall were two very significant events.

I was outside, by the back porch and crossing a small block of stone that we had placed over the old bridal paths to make a tiny bridge to get to the other side. At dusk one night, I saw a black and white cat. It was watching me. When I went toward the cat; it ran. I would call it and occasionally see it from a distance through my window. I would watch the cat investigate my home. It felt safe, I suppose, under that little bridge that crossed the old bridal paths.

She appeared to be a tuxedo cat! Little white paws, white fur that perfectly shaped a vest on her chest a black nose and a bright pink mouth protected by white whiskers. I would notice other cats occasionally running around at dusk and dawn, but she was a tricky one and engaged my attention.

One particular weekend morning, I looked out my bedroom window to my front garden as I usually do in the early hours to begin my morning routine. The front of my house faces east, allowing the sun's rays to reflect on the Shasta daisies and pink poppies that during this time of year lie gently across the white picket fence. This particular morning as I looked out, I saw a new and welcome sight: The Tuxedo Cat with her Tuxedo kitten playing in the garden amongst the sea grass!

Tiny and small yet strong and playful, Tuxedo Cat was teaching her tiny kitten. I silently watched, being careful that she didn't see or hear me. I watched them interact for what seemed like hours. With one paw making the sea grass flutter, her kitten rolled under it, hopped on top of it and hid in between the long green blades. The mother cat finally lay down on top of the soft flat stones to the side of the picket fence to rest. Her kitten came to her. Licking her kitten's fur, she cleaned her tiny baby and while I was observing her, it was apparent to me that Tuxedo Cat was a diligent, caring and protective Mother Cat. So, I named her Mother Cat.

Eventually she noticed me, observing her. I ran downstairs, anxious now to make a connection. I opened one of the doors of the two car garage in the hope that she might want and or need shelter. But then, as quickly as she had arrived, she disappeared!

Secret Ferals or Secret Owners?

I can't tell you when this all began, but at some point, I began to leave a little bowl of food out for Mother Cat that eventually expanded to include a little bowl of Half and Half. You know, the cream that some of us put in our morning coffee. In her initial visits, I was feeding her the cat food that I had left over from Miko. But when the food ran out, and she was back at my door step, hungry and waiting and I had nothing left to give her, Gary, my husband suggested trying the Half and Half and well, discarding the myth of upsetting Mother Cat's tummy by giving her milk products, I set out a small bowl. She loved it! I finally had a little feline friend whose visits I would become increasingly accustomed to.

For a long time, days went on like this. Then one warm summer evening in early June 2006, we had a party at our home, affectionately named Oak Mews by the former owners. We liked to open the main entrance doors to Oak Mews where guests would be greeted upon their arrival.

"Your cat wants to come inside," said one of the hostesses.

"But I don't have a cat," I said in front of all our guests. I felt our secret was revealed. We too, like so many others in Tuxedo Park, had been caring for "a wild feral cat." Surprisingly, not only did this wild feral cat park herself in the middle of the entrance on the driveway to the main door, she ardently brought along two of her pals for the festivities. Toothless Tommy who, I would later learn, was quite the Romeo. He was a gorgeous grey and white tuxedo cat who looked as if he had some partial breed of Persian or Maine coon. There was also a beautiful Black Panther short haired type cat with the most sensitive droopy big round golden eyes. It wasn't too long after all the guests had arrived, that Mother Cat then really made a statement by parking herself inside one of the two urns that outlined the porch entry way. She was looking very comfortable and quite regal! This was the closest she ever had been, and it was agonizing to be missing my chance at an interaction with her.

HIDDEN SPOTS

After a few years, I never ceased wondering—where did Mother Cat go? Where did she stay and sleep at night? My curiosity continued to peak when winter came. I decided I could follow her paw prints and track her. The paw prints would lead me to the direction of the path she took, but not her actual spots.

Behind our home, to the left, up a hill, are old stone structures and designs from the remains of an estate garden. The gardens belonged to a home on Tower Hill Loop where Richard Hunt Howland once lived. Its current owners have done a good job at many attempts to return the gardens to their original grandeur. On this particular occasion, I followed her paw prints deep within these gardens until the snow melted and they were no longer visible. I sensed that Mother Cat was watching me and I continued my search. Eventually I found myself in a place I had never been to before, and that no one else had visited, either, in a very long time. I began to feel a little queasy about being there by myself, as if I was on some desolate adventure in a place I no longer recognized. You could smell the moss and lack of sunlight. The cool dampness hung over me like an old oak tree. I had made it this far, I thought, she may even be watching me from her spot, but I'm not going to back down now. If I were a cat, where would I be?

'Shelter', I thought. I would need to imagine my stealth cat self into those places, spots where predators couldn't get to me. Bramble grew hut like spaces that would make for good protection. As I looked down at one such structure from her path which led me there, I saw things I wish I hadn't. That was enough to turn away, head back home and try to follow her again on another day.

As the seasons changed, the sun melted away most of the snow making it even harder to track her. On one particular day, after Mother Cat ate from my bowl offerings, I decided I was going to follow her again. I needed to know where she went. I anticipated her arrival to my house in the early afternoon as she so often did. Her accuracy in timing was always close to perfect—Another amazing quality felines have. Feeding times were always the same; bedtime was always at 8:30pm and they rose again around 11:00pm. Consistent, felines follow the time of nature. Or-do felines have their own built in sense of time?

Then, just like that, there she was. I saw Mother Cat trotting down a path from the big hill. This is a path that the deer have created. Seasonally, herds of deer follow the same path year to year. I now wonder if this is another spot? Could there be even more shelter and better protection for her up in that direction? I decided I had to find out. With my muck boots on, hat, gloves, and scarf and feeling determined in my full hiking gear, I began my search. Directly behind my home and to the right, I followed her.

Up the deer path, there is a house with stone turrets that neighbors and old timers have referred to as "The Castle." Mother Cat caught me following her up this path and looked startled, as if I wasn't supposed to know where her hidden spots were. I told her "After all these years, I'm going to follow you and I'm determined to know where you go all day!"

I continued to follow her, and she led me to "The Castle" that I've since learned was named Paxhurst. Paxhurst was originally designed in 1904 for William Mitchell Vail Hoffman, and his wife, Irene Stoddard. Since that time, Paxhurst has changed owners several times.

As I approached The Castle through bramble, weeds and no doubt, ticks, Paxhurst loomed colossal in size. The house looked neglected and on closer inspection it was. 'This would be a great place for a cat to shelter its kittens', I thought to myself. When I got closer to the house, there were a set of stone stairs that wound up to what appeared to be a terrace, and then a covered sun room perhaps? From where I stood, it was difficult to tell. But what I could see, as I looked up the stone stairs appeared odd to me. There were large metal cages, typically used to trap raccoons, woodchucks or what some might consider nuisance wild life. Sometimes, these cages would also be used to trap cats. The traps seemed horrifying to me. They appeared to be placed on alternating steps and looked rusty from the passage of time.

I wondered, did Mother Cat have to endure any of those contraptions that clearly had been placed by human hands? It was becoming clearer to me, that a day in the life of cats in Tuxedo Park could be more dangerous and unbearable than I ever would have imagined.

I decided at this point it was unsafe and uncomfortable to stay at The Castle any longer and search for her. There were so many places that she could hide and protect herself, and I felt satisfaction just knowing that would be a strong possibility. I turned around and made my way down the trail back home.

Sheila Pompan

Deep in the Bramble
I ponder the day
Wondering where Felines hide and play
They can walk miles
And always return
To those hands who feed them
Who care in return

A Journal Entry

July 2006

By the end of July 2006, I could clearly see that Mother Cat was pregnant. Waddling a bit, with her bulging tummy, she was beginning to arrive two and three times a day for her treat. Anticipating the arrival of her family and that the weather would be changing from the hot days of summer to the cool winds of fall, I decided that she might want shelter, and began opening the garage door for her. Once inside the garage, there was another door that led into a small mud room where, I decided I could feed her and keep her safe. I had my contractor install a cat door from the garage into the mud room. No luck though, Mother Cat wanted her food on the front porch. She won again! For some time, the long days went on like this. Once again, my curiosity rose and I wondered where she was spending the rest of her time? On this particular occasion, I decide to once again follow her and see where she went. She was ahead of me though and could wiggle her way into brush and small places and simply disappear!

A Journal Entry

August 2006

It's early August and it's been a few weeks since I've seen Mother Cat. In the past, it wasn't unusual for her to come and go but I don't remember her gone for this length of time. Looking for her and awaiting her arrival has become a favorite pastime. Clearly she was eating the food I left out for her. I won't give up hope just yet, maybe she was just, well, being a cat. When I least expect it, she appears and I always feel graced in her presence. I always feel that she's close by, watching me, because whenever our car pulls up the driveway, she will eventually run up the porch and wait for treats. By this time, she had me running to not only the front porch, but the back porch as well. I was still curious on finding where her other "spots" were.

As fall was nearing, I filled my two large entrance urns with bright yellow seasonal mums. One morning when I went downstairs, she was sitting in one of the urns! I quietly examined her from the entrance door window. This was the rare opportunity that I had been waiting for all this time! I ran upstairs and took out my OM1 camera, removed the small lens and replaced it with my zoom. I rushed back to the entrance door window and waited for the right time to begin to shoot. She saw me. She was looking straight into my lens! This was the closest I'd ever been to her. This Mother Cat liked being photographed! She was beautiful. Raw and wild from her outdoor adventures but beautiful knowing that she was carrying new life inside her. She acknowledged me, finally! Her expression was calm and proud. She blinked slowly at me and I blinked back. I felt a very strong connection to her that came from very deep within. I knew she knew that I had gained her trust. My patience had been rewarded. Cats can be tough with acknowledging your existence. Exhausting in fact. But now I had a new project, a higher purpose and a better sense of what it means to be a feral cat.

Mother Cat-During this time period she must have been carrying her kittens

FELINE SURPRISES

October 7, 2006

Fall was unusually warm in 2006. The sun created bold leaf colors and the warm breezes spun the herbs and flowers into an intoxicating fragrance. That year, in particular, I remember the smell of heather and honeysuckle. We spent our weekend mornings in our usual routine, having our morning coffee, catching up on world events and enjoying our favorite pastime, waiting and watching for the arrival of Mother Cat. I suspected she'd been watching me from her "secret spot." After several hopeful walks to the porch, and several cups of coffee, bingo! There she was, and, she was not alone!

"Oh no!" I gasped, trying to keep quiet so I wouldn't frighten her. I tiptoed to the kitchen calling out to Gary, in a hushed voice so that I wouldn't startle Mother Cat and make her run away, yet brimming with excitement and wanting to share this little miracle of happiness with him!

"Come, come quick, be quiet, walk softly, and hurry." There at the front door on our porch sat Mother Cat, looking up at the window at us, with her chest high and her stature proud. She brought not one, not two, but three little kittens with her to our porch. Three tiny little kittens! The view from our entrance door was nothing short of miraculous. We felt honored at the sight. These three tiny puffs of innocent fur looked up at us experiencing their latest adventure with expressions of expectations that only their Mother Cat could have conveyed to them. "Here we are," they said. I now understand why she had been away for so long.

The first kitten that stood out to both of us was this tiny little grey and white tuxedo kitten who looked directly at us with two large round golden colored eyes. You could feel the boldness, the courage and even the sense of entitlement of this small creature. Mother Cat looked proud! I mean we could feel how proud she was to introduce us to her three tiny little kittens of life, her gifts, all the way from her special spot on a journey to visit us. Us! You could feel it from her as she looked at them and looked at us with an expression that neither of us saw or felt before.

We wondered if she waited for us to arrive for the weekend and was this their first journey and adventure out into the world? Had she been waiting until they were strong enough on their own for her to show them off to us? It was thrilling. Smiles galore! The other two kittens were black. One had a little white spot on its chest with diamond-shaped eyes that had a slight shade of aqua. The other kitten was very very small with a black coat, white fur in its ears and big round light blue eyes. Its little head tilted to its side as it gazed up at us through the window as if trying to understand who we were and what this was all about? It was these distinctive features on each of the kittens that would help me tell them apart during the course of their visits. Their eye color indicated to me how young they must have been. Gary and I laughed because we knew exactly who their fathers had been. Toothless Tommy and Panther Cat with the big round eyes! Recollections of Mother Cat's unusually friendly behavior the evening of our party in early June entered both of our minds! Cats can gestate with multiple fathers, something I never knew until this experience.

Ok, well now I have three kittens and a Mother Cat to take care of. Interaction, purpose, excitement! I'm feeling life again! Gary immediately thought she wanted me to feed them. "There so tiny," I said. "Give them Half and Half," Gary said, "like you've been giving Mother Cat." I told myself that milk might upset their stomachs, but then again Mother Cat had been lapping up the Half and Half for months. Besides, it's all that I had for them. I'd have to get KMR, kitten food, I thought. But in the meantime, let me retrieve three small bowls so that I could properly feed them.

While rummaging through miniature plates and bowls I thought, they're too little for individual servers, how about a big plate so they can all stay together? Yes, I think quickly, what do I have? I find a large plastic round platter with individual compartments for each of their portions. Perfect! First I pour myself some Half and Half into my final cup of coffee and pour the remainder into three of the compartments and a separate bowl for the Mother Cat. I walk quietly to the front porch so as not too startle them. Ok, how do I do this?

I'm so excited to meet them. Mother Cat sees me through the front door window. I show her the bowl and platter and acknowledge her with the usual cat greeting of blinking eyes slowly. I carefully open the door; she brings her kittens to the third step, farthest from the door as she stays on the first. Slowly and quietly I open the door. I place the bowl and platter down in her usual spot and begin to speak to her; she gave me a short low growl in return as a warning to keep my distance. She scared me and I almost spilled everything but I didn't. I intended to feed those kittens and get to know them! I closed the door, heart beating and feeling kind of hurt that she did that.

'This is a darn Cat' I tell myself! You're afraid of a Cat?

If you've ever met an outdoor cat protecting her young, it indeed can be a little frightening. After all, I had already invested so much in her. I respected that there would be no introductions to her kittens that day, but I knew that there would be, eventually. It was on that morning, October 7, 2006, that I was becoming closer to understanding what it meant to be a Feral Cat!

Bernie peeking out at us behind Mums

Sheila Pompan

Mr. Grey, Bernie, Little One, Mother Cat

Mother Cat always keeps a watchful eye on her kittens.
Mr. Grey and Bernie wrestle while Little One lounges in the sun.

Mother Cat and Kittens take a well deserved rest.

Bernie always trying

Bernie on an adventure

Mother Cat and Grey in pot, Bernie wants to join

Mr. Grey in his signature pose

Strike a Pose

Sheila Pompan

Buddies

THE SCAR ON HER FACE

She didn't lose an eye, proof she put up a good fight. Proof that nothing would come into harm's way of her kittens. Her scar initially shocked us, but it also stood as a reminder to any human and perhaps predator who saw her, that those kittens were her property, and a signal to keep their distance from them. It was a fresh wound when she first brought her kittens to us that warm fall day in October. The scar was just above her right eye. It told a story. Her intention, I felt, was to focus on her kittens, not her wound that eventually would heal on its own. This also gave us the indication that she was healthy and hopeful that she was not feline leukemia positive, as so many assume most feral cats to be.

I will always remember those touching moments of the tiny grey kitten licking his Mother Cat's wound. Another reminder of their strong natural instincts to take care of each other. There are hidden rituals in the animal kingdom that we may never witness. My observations allowed me into their world for which I feel fortunate to have observed on so many occasions.

I have always wondered if it were human hands that injured her. There was something about where the wound was and how it looked. It's no wonder she taught diligent lessons to her kittens that humans were to be feared. Humans have behaved horrifically to our animal kingdom. There appears to be a natural instinct and bond amongst animals and their newborns that if broken before its natural time can have disastrous results for the offspring as well as for the parents. The animal kingdom can teach us so much, if only we took time to observe them, to try and connect their fears with behaviors they so often are forced to show us.

Being a Mother Cat is hard Work.

Mother Cat teaching her Kittens

Scar on her face

A Hay Home for Kittens

As time went on, she made my front porch their home. I placed some hay in one of the urns. I was reading everything I could to learn about feral kittens and cats. As the seasons were changing, I learned that hay made a good bed for them. I had never purchased hay before. I went to my local country garden shop and asked how much was a bale of hay? The proprietor said $5.00. I said, "I'll take two bales, please." He asked me to pull my car around and that he'd put them into the car for me. I told him I didn't need help and he smiled and said I'll meet you, round back. I thought to myself "what great service and what a nice guy."

When I pulled up to the back, he was standing there with the first bale of hay.

'Oh my gosh,' I thought to myself, 'I had no idea a bale of hay was so big.' One definitely would have been enough. Would the other one even fit into the car? The nice service man got it inside my car and waved me goodbye. 'Oh gosh,' I'm thinking, 'the inside of my car is going to be a mess from all this hay. On the way home I began sneezing my head off! Oh gosh, could I be allergic to cats and hay?'

I pulled up the driveway and opened the back of the car. The bales were wrapped with twine but oh boy did I purchase two too many. Well, I told myself, 'let's get these new hay homes ready for these kittens. From all that I'd read, I also learned about various methods of creating homes for our outdoor feline friends. I made little homes from Styrofoam coolers. I taped the top portion to the body of the cooler and then cut a round hole into the body for their entry. I placed some hay inside. I set them in various spots in my garage and named the homes "Cat Mews." From there, I graduated to the pet stores and found small covered fleece bedding, which the grey kitten immediately took as his. I created little tunnels and nests for each of them within the bails of hay. My allergies were at an all time high but the kittens were warm and safe!

From everything I'd read, ferals are wild outdoor cats and rarely are able to be domesticated. If, on the very rare occasion that this does happen, these cats will typically become extremely attached to their owners. Clearly the point was made however, with everything that I read, that I shouldn't get my hopes up too high to inherit an indoor kitty. Gary on the other hand was convinced that they would be sleeping inside and at the end of our bed in no time. I was not so convinced. And as for Mother Cat, she was already out dating, and with new "cats" that I hadn't seen around before. It was time to bring in an expert.

"I'll take care of them just until spring arrives then they'll be strong enough to be on their own"

JUST UNTIL SPRING ARRIVES

On bales of hay.

Do the Right Thing!

Mother Cat was quite clever. It appeared the cat door to the mudroom was useful after all. By the time Thanksgiving came and then Christmas, my feline family was quite safe inside our garage with a cat door entry into the mud room. Eventually, I was getting them to eat inside the kitchen, but Mother Cat wasn't happy about that and she would let me know without hesitation.

Good fortune was once again bestowed on my feline family and January and February of 2007 proved to be a very mild winter. Mother cat was creating a new habit of bringing an unkempt surly looking character into the mudroom to chow. On one particular occasion, our painter, who has taken care of our endless home projects over the years and has observed and participated in my many Tuxedo cat adventures, was helping me wall paper and re finish a pair of doors original to the house when Mother Cat brought her new friend around. He saw this bedraggled looking character and said, "I know that cat, he lives up there on Crows Nest Road where the doctor lives."

"The Doctor?" I said.

"Yes, the psychiatrist," he said. Being a psychology major with my own desires to be a therapist in the early stages of my career, I'm always interested in hearing about those people who actually continued with the profession. I'm fascinated with their patience and listening skills for the duration of 45 minute intervals from the rotation of patients that one must see on any typical day. In any event, initially I doubted my painter because Crows Nest Road is quite far from my house, and I was unable to place the house he was referring to.

"I do work up there all the time," my painter said. That guy has lots of cats that he feeds out back." A colony of cats! I thought this to be very exciting. I've only read about cat colonies and never actually saw on.

"How many are there?" I asked.

"A lot, and I know I've seen that dark grey one many times. He's the head cat up there, what they call the Alpha cat."

"I still find it hard to believe they would travel so far." Where is this house again?"

"It's the famous Glass House on Crows Nest Road."

Astonished by the mysterious legacy of these felines I was barely audible in my response; "Oh the Glass House, that's where Loomis once lived."

And this is when my patience wore thin and I decided it was time to turn on the switch to my prefrontal cortex and ignite my CEO lobe! I needed to listen to the executive functioning portion of my brain cells. It was, time to bring in a veterinarian and quell Mother Cat's urges, or we would have stray males in heat and an endless series of pregnancies. Adorable as kittens are, I knew the responsible agenda was to halt indiscriminate breeding for cats and kittens.

When I called the vet who took care of Miko, he absolutely without reservation refused to have an office visit with a feral cat. I was appalled! "These are my cats and I've been taking care of them for months!"

Thankfully, that was not the last word. There is a group of human feline friends who pull together should this type of information become necessary. I knew about the wonderful spay/neuter release program that California promoted and had learned more about it through research and a dear friend who lives in Morro Bay. However, I couldn't find many programs here in the Northeast. In fact, information was surprisingly scarce.

I'm not clear how it happened, probably from another miraculous intervention, but I heard about a wonderful woman named Carolyn Roberts who helps with strays and ferals in Tuxedo Park and would be knowledgeable and could aid me in this regard. Again, I had to be cautious about introducing myself as a cat keeper, since many people who kept feral cats here didn't want anyone to know what they were doing. I called Carolyn Roberts and introduced myself and explained my situation. We spoke several times on the phone before we met. I told her about my spay/neuter release plan, believing at the time in the myth that I didn't have any other alternative, because these cats had been labeled "wild and dangerous"!

Carolyn Roberts said she would be happy to help me. I invited her over to my home so we could meet and she could help me with the steps I needed to take to trap them. (I shudder when I even write that word) On the day she pulled up the driveway, Mother Cat and her kittens were in the pot, just as they had been when they arrived in October 2006. Carolyn very quietly closed the car door and got out of her car. The first thing she said was "they're not feral." By the end of our meeting we determined that they were semi-feral. She would walk me through the steps of captures, Have-a-Heart cages and early morning encouragement. I was very uncomfortable doing this. The very thought of hearing that trap door clunk down filled me with anxiety. I had read so many stories about trapping and how perfectly accurate it had to be; else the results could have dire consequences. But who, I asked myself, who would spay and neuter my little fellows?

Carolyn said she knew just the vet who could do the job, and introduced us to a veterinarian who never hesitated when I called her about my "feral cats." Rather, her response was, "bring them in when you' have them and we'll make room." There was no need for an appointment, which logically would have been nearly impossible to make. She also assisted me with the process of trapping them, which felt far from natural to me. But when Mother Cat brought that other unkempt character through the cat door into my mudroom, I just knew I was doing the right thing and that I would not be able to keep up the pace of properly caring for her and her projected three to four annual litters.

When the time came, everything went smoothly and calmly. Well at least for the Mother Cat, who I was most concerned about, and the two black kittens. The small cute and least suspecting wild kitten, the kitten who captured our hearts because of his stunning looks, turned out to have strength well beyond his seemingly tiny stature. Grey kitten was mad and it showed in his tiny face and eyes.

On January 15, 2007 Mother Cat was spayed, Mr. Grey was neutered January 16, 2007 and Bernie on January 19, 2007. Little One was spayed on the same day as Bernie, January 19, 2007. It was on these dates that we discovered we had two males and a female. Finally, we could give them their official names! From these dates forward, our family included Mr. Grey, Little One and Bernie.

As far as the whereabouts of Alpha grey cat, we never did see him again. Perhaps he stayed put at the Glass House or found another Loomis house to roam to, where his feline urges proved more useful.

THE RELEASE

A Journal Entry
May 9, 2007

Today Bernie and Mr. Grey went outside for the first time alone, without Mother Cat. December 2006 was the last time they had been outside. With reservation I opened the garage door for them, while their perplexed faces watched me, anticipating what would be on the other side. Bernie went towards the great outdoors first. He gave me a reassuring look over his shoulder, and with reserve yet enthusiastically with his tail up, he dashed out first while Mr. Grey watched in a crouched down position. Then slowly he raised himself looked up at me and followed Bernie. They returned to all their familiar spots. First, they went to the side of the house, past the white picket fence down the small hill to the back porch. Mr. Grey began to pant before he reached the back porch, but he continued to follow Bernie. They climbed trees and let out all their pent-up winter energy. Mr. Grey chucked up two hairballs. Little One stayed sleeping inside somewhere, I think in her spot in the tool room. Bernie and Mr. Grey were having a great time. I watched with careful eyes from both outside and inside. Mr. Grey let out a howl and then chucked up two more hairballs. I will never forget how proud I was of them. Bernie was strong. He leaped up a big oak tree as if he had been working out his muscles all winter long. He went from a kitten to an adult cat right before my eyes. Mr. Grey on the other hand followed along, but once up in that tree, he needed coaxing from me on how to get down.

They continued their adventures as I watched them from my camera lens. I tried to allow them their freedom, their independence. I knew Mother Cat had prepared them well, and by keeping them safe inside from the cold winter months, I had convinced myself that they would be released, back to where they came from. I knew they wouldn't go far. When Bernie saw my camera, he began to show off. It turned into a photo session of sorts. Not so much about releasing them to the great outdoors, but rather, "let me show off in front of our human Mom and have her take a lot of pictures of us." Eventually I went inside and let it be.

By dusk, Mr. Grey popped back into the kitchen. He ate and went straight into his donut bed. I gently went over to him with his brush and comb and examined him for ticks or anything else that may have been unusual. He had his shots so I knew he was protected. He looked good. I gave him a brushing and he went into his usual cute pose on his back. He was in dreamland. So much for independence and the great outdoors! Little One strolled by, and after smelling his new outdoor odor, she ran upstairs to the yellow room and wanted nothing more from her brothers' new outdoor adventure.

It was a few weeks later when Bernie arrived home. I saw him running from the back of the house to our back door, as if he was going to rejoin the family with a lot of cat tales to tell. He always has been able to make me smile with his aura of entitlement. I have never been able to be mad at Bernie. Even when on more than one occasion, he created some shenanigans.

He trotted back inside when I opened the door. At first glance, I saw a change in his face, I saw his father! His nose had grown longer and wider, his chest had filled out and his tail was longer. He looked like an adult cat. It took me back for a few seconds.

Once inside, he felt right at home and began cleaning himself in his donut bed. But not so fast, said his siblings. When they saw him, the little one hissed at him, and Mr. Grey, usually the stable easy going one did the same thing. Bernie was clearly hurt. He hung his head down. They sniffed him and wouldn't let him near the food bowl they had all been sharing since they were kittens. A new behavior.

I stood back and observed. I brought Bernie upstairs to a bathroom and placed him in the sink. I began brushing him and examining his claws, his coat, and his ears. To my surprise, he loved it! To my bigger surprise, I found several ticks on his neck. This was new for me too. I researched what to do and did it. To my great astonishment, Bernie the cat, my wonderful, wonderful cat sat patiently as I removed each and every tick with a tweezers and carefully placed it in rubbing alcohol for removal. I gave him a good brush, and lots of hugs. He slept that night with us in his usual spot.

Within a few days, Bernie smelled like the rest of the family and was once again in his natural order with his siblings. The balance of life as we knew it was once again restored. All was well and my idea of releasing them to the great outdoors was unanimously voted "no." They had no further interest in returning outside, except to view it from the windows, inside their cozy, comfy abode.

Back outdoors. Vaccinated and Neutered. Spring 2007

Mr. Grey's signature pose

Teenagers

Spring 2007! Bernie now looks like his father.

A Journal Entry

August 30, 2007

There are secret spots for feline friends
Places they return to
Spots that are safe havens
For mother cats to leave their young one's.

It's been just about a year since their birth and they return to those secret spots. Finding comfort, familiarity and perhaps waiting for their birth mother to return. For just a quick glimpse or the return of a cat dance. Those familiar rituals of bunting heads and licking faces.

For Mom, she wants them to find their own "spots." She claimed these outdoor spots as belonging to her long ago. To her, it's only natural that they find their own spots too.

She stares them down through the window now,
As they sit up high
On their perches inside.

June 2007 - Last photo taken of Mother Cat.

THE COUNTRY CATS OF TUXEDO PARK

In Their Own Words

Hello. My name is Mr. Grey. I'm the responsible leader of this feline family with a generally well-rounded disposition and very much deserving of my title and surname. I'm also the spokescat for my feline siblings to our human family. My Feline Mum placed me in charge of my siblings when I was just a wee kitten. I have a very even temperament. I'm a fast learner; I learned my hunting skills quickly and eagerly. I stayed by my Mother Cat's side until she finally got a little angry with me and wanted me to move along on my own. I'm extremely loyal, and a great buddy. I love to be brushed and groomed, even including nail clippings. Something most cats loath and will take a flying leap to avoid.

Some of my favorite activities include chasing feet and toes under the sheets and blankets when it's bedtime, mussing the sheets when my human owner is making up the beds, sitting with my human parents on their laps or performing tricks, like sitting on their backs while making them walk around with me still perched. I really love being rocked while laying upside down on my human mother's legs as she sings to me. I love the herbs from my human Mum's garden. We have the same routine whenever she's out there collecting her variety of herbs to cook with. I run, tail up to the window where I can view her perfectly, and repeat a loud meow to remind her to bring something back inside for me. When she's on her way back to the house she'll always stop and greet me at the window and show me what she's got. That gets me very excited and with tail up I jump down from the window and run to the door and greet her. Then I stretch up high on my hind paws and reach into her herb basket with my front paws to smell what she brought back for me. That's one of our favorite rituals. I also enjoy playing with the husk when they bring home corn on the cob. My human mum always ends up shucking it when I begin to play with it.

If my human Mum isn't getting up in the morning when I'm ready, I'll place my paw under her camisole strap and snap it until she becomes really irritated and this will get her up! If that doesn't work then I'll nip at Gary's calves, or any exposed skin. This is a behavior taught by our Mother Cat to encourage us to do something that we didn't want to do. It doesn't hurt but it sure is annoying.

My favorite times of day are morning when everyone is getting up and dinner time when the food is being prepared. They let me sit on the counter and watch the activities. I like it when the fireplace is flaming and flickering and everyone is lounging together. I love my Buddie Bernie and I ease the tension between Bernie and my sister, Little One. I always want to be a part of whatever is going on... I have lots of windows here at the Country House and I love lounging on my kittie condo and watching the birds, the squirrels, the seasonal wild turkeys, the occasional black bear, the woodchucks and especially the chipmunks. They're active little creatures especially in the morning.

I have a unique and consistent hello greeting where I lay on my side, twist my back paws up over my head and lay on my back to show you how happy I am that you're here. I was also the first one to bunt heads with my human Mum. When I displayed that affectionate ritual towards her, my siblings followed and we never wanted to go outside again.

Little One, AKA Tootsie, Tina or Mabel

Hi. I've been called by many different names. Most of the time they call me Little One, but they also call me Tootsie, or Tina or Mabel. Bernie and I were pals as kittens. We played together all the time, but that changed as we matured. We would bunt heads and he'd kiss me but later he'd trick me and begin to stalk me. I still fall for it every time. We tolerate each other. I'm very very shy. I have a tiny timid meow that my Human Mom will always respond to with great enthusiasm. My human owners say I'm sweet. I enjoy being brushed and groomed. Mr. Grey escorts me to my food bowl and litter box. He's a great protector and I feel safe with him. I like playing with my human Mom when he's around. I'm learning to become more independent. I'm grateful my human parents kept me and I have lots of surprises in store for them in the near future.

Hey there, they call me Bernie. Cool name for me. I like it a lot. It's short for Bernard, the middle name of my human owner. They say I was the runt of the litter. My human owners used to keep an extra watch for me when I was a kitten. I was always the last one to be given attention by my feline Mom. Small as I was, I always had an adventurous nature, and my feline Mom would always be able to find me, even when I didn't come when I was called with a strong meow.

My human parents like to tell stories about me when I was the runt. Like the time there was a big storm coming. The wind was blowing leaves all around. As usual I was the last one to get picked up, but after awhile being alone under the porch, one of our many secret spots, I decided to venture up to the top of the porch where I could be seen. My human parents saw me and became worried when the wind blew me over. I got right up again of course, but they decided that a can of food might just lure me inside where they felt I'd be safer. When they stepped out to get me, my feline Mom ran to me, picked me up and brought me to the rest of our feline family to another secret spot. I had another close call when Rocky the dog, who liked to come running down the hill from his house and scare us, got a little too close. Yet I always knew where the "hiding spots" were and was able to get to safety on my very own. I could climb trees too before my siblings even tried. They watched; I climbed. Mr. Grey decided to follow me once but he didn't know how to get down. Eventually he did descend backwards after watching me shimmy and leap down but when he tried the maneuver he ended up with a hernia that needed repair.

Eventually, I matured into a loyal, loving, snuggly feline with my human owners, especially my human Mom. I pushed for her attention and always won. I love being groomed and lying with her when she's reading, watching the tube, working or feels cold and needs some furry body heat to warm her. I'm the one who sleeps between my human parents when they're in dreamland. If they have to get up, my job is to escort them.

One of my many unique qualities is tilting my head to the side when I'm trying to learn something new or when I'm trying to understand you. I also enjoy sleeping on my back with my front paws tucked into my chest and my back haunches relaxed and spread, flat to the floor. This pose is a great attention-getter and photo opportunity to compensate for the lack of photos of me as a kitten. Sometimes Mr. Grey will join in next to me and our human Mom will start taking photos of us. She thinks we don't know she's there but we have a keen sense of everything. Sometimes we stir and strike other cute poses and she'll stay with us even longer.

"Look, Gary, look they're so cute."

One of our favorite heart catchers is being on our backs with our front paws over our eyes. When I become really relaxed and in the Zen state, the tip of my little pink tongue will show and my human parents will really coo over me.

More favorite activities: playing airplane scissors with my human Mom's fingers, batting the toy mouse on a string (I'm a pretty good batter) chasing the red laser pointer, lapping up everyone's Half and Half, a habit from kittenhood, watching my human Mom work out, sitting between her legs while she's trying to stretch, watching her meditate, playing in the middle of the night with Gary, watching him snore or purr or whatever that sound is he makes, mousing, watching birds and chipmunks from all our windows, hangin with my bud Mr. Grey, terrorizing the Little One, (I have never and would never harm her), putting my smell on Gary when he doesn't want me to and walking across the computer keys when I'm not getting the attention I want. I love laying in high places such as the book shelves, cabinets and the windows in the kitchen.

I'm not cooperative when I have to travel but my human family can't resist my adventurous, energetic and delightful spirit and everyone loves me to pieces. I'm not very vocal; I don't need to be, but when I am, I would fall into the baritone vocal range. I don't miss a beat of life. I like to run and jump into high places such as the kitchen cabinets and the windowsill high above it all. From up there, I can see some cool birds. I have the run of the house and can play when you least expect it, as when you're sleeping or snoring. Overall, I'm a sensitive dude and can feel the love of the household.

INTERVIEWS WITH THE CATS:

Bernie: Well now that you met us and know a little something about us, let us tell you something about our human Mom.

Mr. Grey: I was the first one to do the head bunt with her and stay inside, let me tell it.

Little One: Meow, why don't we all tell it?

Bernie: Ok, but I'll start. Our human Mom had cats all of her life with all the typical names, Bootsie, Snowball, Boolli, and oh yes, Miko, the cat with the big shoes to fill. A Calico, a female feline.

Mr. Grey: Evidently, it wasn't until I looked straight into our human Mums eyes for the very first time that she felt my humanness, apparently startling her. It was at this very moment that she knew she would keep us forever.

Little One: We should thank our Feline Mother for bringing us to our human household. She knew Miko went to the Rainbow Bridge and that our human Mom needed us as much as we would need her.

Bernie and Mr. Grey: Meooow, Meeow, mee, we had a great feline mother! Myaw Mu Meow, Meooow Mu Mother Cat.

Bernie: Ok then, that was a good idea Little One. One point for you!

Little One: Mi!

Bernie: Now, back to our human Mom. Our human Mom is kind and very, very patient, qualities we would need to survive. She may not have been up for the task if not for our other human owner, Gary. He saw how cute we were and said "Let's keep em."

Little One: Yeah that's right Bernie, it was him, when Mother Cat brought us to the porch for the first time.

Mr. Grey: Dear Ones, it was all because of me that any of us have the life we do. He took one look at me and said, "Look at that cute little grey one," I hooked him in upon his first view of me when I gazed directly into his human eyes.

Bernie: No, no, it was me, man, it was my smallness.

Little One: No it was all of us, Mi!

Bernie: Anyway, she's the best human Mom ever. She sings songs all the time to us, like this one, "You are my sunshine, my only sunshine,"

Little One: Bernie it's up an octave, like this; You make me happy, when skies are gray. Mr. Grey joins in – "you'll never know, dears, how much I love you, please don't take, my sunshines' away"!

Bernie: I have my own song she sings to me; Bernie the cat, the wonderful wonderful cat.

Little One: Bernie you're off key, and please go up an octave, she's not that low.

Mr. Grey: May I suggest we let our owners tell the rest of the story? It may just move along a little faster.

Bernie: Mooah.

Little One: Mi!

COUNTRY CATS, BIG CITY- THE CAT FAMILY TRIES APARTMENT LIFE

The air smelled different here and so was the view when we first arrived. She placed our carriers on the floor. She let us rest for awhile after our car ride.

Wow, let's explore, said Bernie. "Look at those kitty condos, and our very own food dishes. "Quick, come back here guys, a litter box, two of them."

"I like this linen closet, said the Little One. Come back in here; let's check out our new kitty condo. Wow, look at these windows"!

"Where are all the trees?" said Mr. Grey."

"And the birds," said Bernie.

"Look below you, are those birds, the yellow speedy ones? said Little One.

"I believe those are the same kind of animal that got us here," replied Mr. Grey.

Our human Mom opens the big long windows just enough for us to smell the air. It smells really different here," says Bernie.

"Yeah, I don't smell the trees or the grass or our herb garden," states Mr. Grey. "I like all this sunshine" says Little One. "Yeah, that's cool," says Bernie. "Let's go check out where our human Mom went, she's back in this other room. Wow, look at where they sleep. This will be big enough for all of us to be together."

"And look at all the sunlight," says Little One.

Our human Mom picks us up and puts us on a windowsill, facing North. Little One runs away. Look there, boys, there are your trees. We call it Central Park.

"Whoa, what's that?" asks Bernie.

"It's called a pigeon."

"Are they always this close to the window?" asks Mr. Grey. Well you see, boys, they like to get away from all the hustle and bustle that you see below. Windowsills are a great place for that. Similar to your spots in the country. I'm going to unpack the rest of your things. All of this is for you to explore. "I'm following you," says Bernie.

"I'm going to stay on this sill a little longer. Nah, I'm coming with you guys," says Mr. Grey.

Little One returns and follows her brothers, "Wait for me!"

I kept them in the city for several months that year. Bernie and Mr. Grey loved their kitty condos and made our red suede tomato swivel chair one of their favorite spots. While Little One enjoyed early mornings under the stair master practicing her batting skills with a red ribbon that hung on the handle for her. She also found more comfort and less stimulation in the small linen closet, which she preferred. Mr. Grey settled into a chair of his own after dinner time and when it came to close our eyes and fall asleep, there was indeed enough room on that oversized fluffy bed for all of us.

I found Honeywell industrial-sized air filters to curb my allergies and we all enjoyed the herb garden from our terrace that year. Catnip for them and tomatoes and basil for us!

"We never saw a sunset before," said Bernie. Our human Mom put us on the windowsill facing west, so we could experience it for the very first time. There were so many different shades of color."

Little One watched from the door that led to the terrace while we sat on the window sill above her. "Meooow!" As shades of color changed and the warm air turned cooler, we saw lots of bright fireflies. And when we looked down below us, even the yellow birds had fireflies attached to them. Yet somehow there was something different about these fireflies than the fireflies at home.

In this place our human parents called the city, our ears were wiggling from all the new sounds too. *Beeps,* long long sounds that would be heard all hours of the night. It wasn't the familiar sounds we heard in the country from our canine friends, or the seasonal turkey family in the fall, or the whistling sound of hawks or the beautiful songs from cardinals, blue birds, finches and all our other flying friends. These noises happened every evening when we could best see what was going on behind the big windows. Our human Mom eventually explained these flashing lights weren't fireflies or birds. She explained to us that what we called birds was actually the same type of contraption that brought us here from our country home, called cars and taxi cabs, and what we thought were fireflies here, they called lights and that unlike the country, we could see and hear them throughout the evening until the sun rose the following morning.

We loved watching these new toys from our windowsill."

"I could do without all the sounds said Mr. Grey," it's interfering with my cat centeredness."

"Me too, said Little One." "Sometimes our human Mom would want us to go out in the hall. She said something about getting exercise. But whenever we heard "*ding*," we learned that a slow *swoosh* could be heard followed by the appearance of unknown humans."

"We didn't like that and we would all go racing down the hall back into our home of safety." She always said, "Good, now you got your exercise."

Hey Bernie, remember the time you didn't run when you heard that *ding* and walked toward that swoosh?" "Oh boy do I ever Grey. Human Mom came after me just as the *swoosh* sound was ending and I almost couldn't see her anymore." I watched from the other side of this thing as her hand, the one that brushes us, allowed me to run out of that spot and back to you guys. I remember her tones telling us not to go in there. I think she called it celuator, ventulator."

"Nooo, Bernie," replied Little One, she said L IV A TOR."

In their red swivel chair.

Our place in the city.

Sheila Pompan

Hangin in NYC

Back to the Country
Where we Belong,
In that contraption,
We all squeeze along.
Finally sounds and smells we once knew,
Remind us we're home,
Shades of green are the hues.

THEY REMEMBER

Journal Entry
August 5, 2008

I brought our feline family back to the house after spending many months in the city. As we drove closer into the Park, I opened the windows and allowed the once-familiar smells and sounds of the country to return, to be absorbed. As we pulled up the hill of our driveway, the stones crunching beneath the tires offered a much needed calmness after the stressful trip of highways and beeping cars travelling at great speeds.

I carried their carriers from the car to the kitchen. Already, Mr. Grey was recognizing familiar smells and sites. His eyes became brighter and his curiosity peaked. He knew this was his first home.

I brought them upstairs to the yellow room. Mr. Grey first, then Bernie and Little One. Immediately, when the doors of their individual carriers opened, they ran under the bed. I had set the room up with water and food and spread their blanket out on the floor with their brush and toys. I left the room for about twenty minutes. When I returned, Mr. Grey was sitting in the window. He jumped down and greeted me with his familiar upside down roll. He was purring louder than I've heard him in a very long time. He rolled over on his back and meowed for a belly rub. Sitting on the floor with him, he danced around me stroking my ankles and arms and purring with great enthusiasm. He found one of his former mouse toys and brought it to his blanket after batting it across the shiny oak floors. Mr. Grey ate, drank his water and checked out the litter box. He was happy, he remembered, this was his first home. His kitten-like behavior made me wonder, 'did he think he was going to see Mother Cat?" I asked myself, "could the familiar surroundings and smells trigger his kitten- like behavior, or did he actually believe he would reunite with her?" They were the closest of the pack.

For certain, Mr. Grey remembered this home. As far as Bernie and Little One, we'll have to wait for them to wake up to find out!

And soon the trees grew tall and wide
No longer now could you see the sky
Lakes have turned green
Walls have come down
Roadways are blocked
Smiles are now frowns
Humans and animals want to survive
Compete in the Village that once was their pride
Storms have blown through
Nature has shown
That she is in charge
We are not here alone!
9/10/2014

REMARKABLE WORKS OF PASSION

Good fortune once again graced Mother Cat, her kittens and this is where I include myself. For without this next stroke of luck, this story would perhaps never be told or have a very different outcome.

Every once in awhile, you run into those people who are living from their hearts. They do what other people won't or can't. They don't want anything in return and they exceed the bell curve in how they actively live and what they can do for others. Dr Carol Jean Roshkind, from Central Valley Animal Hospital is one of those rare veterinarians and human beings. As I said previously, if not for her, this story may not have existed. What she has done for the ferals, strays and people just like me has had a rippling effect that otherwise would result in very different outcomes for all included. Not only has she slowed down the population growth of strays and our other animal friends who would otherwise be deemed not worth saving, but she has also allowed our animal friends and their owners to enjoy loving, joyful relationships and lives.

For me, this has also become personal. My three "Wild Feral Cats," are a perfect example of what life can be for both pets and their owners, when a Veterinarian makes a decision to spay/neuter and examine our feline friends who otherwise may have been deemed as not worth saving. My three, Mr. Grey, Little One and Bernie, have been the smartest, most loyal, nurturing, loving lap cats that I've ever had. Bernie in particular, considered the runt of the litter, has been the most energetic, adventurous, loving and curious spirit of the three. He came a long way from his early beginnings, and there were some adjustments initially, but Bernie has wanted to please right from the start. He may have taken his sister out on some adventures and created some shenanigans initially, but he is the snuggler of the three and my right hand pal. He's always there and, it would appear, that he understands most of what I'm saying to him and to the others. Always curious, he can be a bit nosey too, continuously wanting to check out everyone and everything. Even, when he's not always invited. He doesn't miss a beat. He's our energetic sensitive boy who we love to pieces. Bernie along with his siblings have added immeasurable joy and love to our home, which otherwise would have been a very quiet, dull and boring household. Trainable you ask? You bet! They won't even jump over a pet gate that separates a formal room from the rest of the house. Their communication skills are to be admired and they listen very well. They understand all of my tones. Most of all, they simply want to please and be a part of our family household. Our home would be sorely different without our feline family.

It is with sincere appreciation and enormous gratitude that our feline family has been under the care of Dr. Carol Roshkind and we will always be thankful to our neighbor Carolyn Roberts for introducing us to this uniquely dedicated Veterinarian. Dr. Carol Roshkind has always been available to provide her professional expertise, kindness, compassion and humane treatment to our feline family members. She has been the right vet for us.

Sometime in July 2014

"Bernie I know you're aware of the lump I found on your neck. I'm sorry you were so stressed when I took you to the Vet."

"I'm a feline and it doesn't feel natural to us. I know you had to do it."

"It appears to be growing too. I want to make the least invasive and most comfortable decision for you."

"That's a human thing, I can't help you with that decision. Humans make decisions all the time for animals. I know that you'll make your decision with empathy and compassion. You're a great owner."

"Thank you Bernie." You've been the best pet I've ever had."

"Your welcome. Would you brush me now?

Hey Bernie, says Little One, "What's that lump on your neck? Did you get that from the tick that you've been carrying around? Huh Bernie what is that?"

"Oh come over here Little sister and let me give you a good stroke and a couple of head bunts."

"Gee Bernie thanks! Why are you suddenly being so nice to me, or is this one of your tricks and your going to chase me into the linen closet again?" Please don't chase me Bernie, I like you better when you're nice like this. It reminds me of when we were kittens."

"Listen Little One, Tootsie, Mabel… from now on you can have free reign of the house." I'll even let you come on my condo. And, you can come inside the downstairs sunroom whenever you want to. No more blocking you."

"Gee Bernie really?"

"Yes really, Little One. You're the only sister I'll ever have and I will always love you and watch over you."

"What do you mean Bernie? You sound like your going away, where are you going Bernie?"

"Little One, you know how I always enjoyed having adventures right? Well think of this as another one of those adventures." Little One stares and blinks at Bernie appearing not to understand what he's saying. "Ah come here Little One and let me walk you downstairs to my kitty condo. I promise I won't stalk you or trick you anymore. Let's go, race ya, on your mark, get set, go"!

EARLY AUGUST 2014

Mr. Grey: Hey buddie how you doing today?

Bernie: Ah so so.

Mr. Grey: Keep drinking the water human Mum left out for you in all your favorite spots. Hey Bernski, would you do something for me?

Bernie: Sure Grey anything.

Mr. Grey: There are many legends and stories about the journey to the heavy side layer on which you're going to cross. Well, I hear that you may be able to meet up with my father, Toothless Tommy. Would you give him a message from me?

Bernie: Of course I will Grey. And if what they say about this journey is true, that means I'll see our feline Mom again too! What message would you like me to give to her?

Mr. Grey: You can tell her what a wonderful feline Mother she was and about the adventures we've been having here in Tuxedo Park. I bet she'll love hearing all about them. And wait until your feline father see's you all grown up Bernie, he's going to recognize you right away because you look just like him! I bet they'll all be there to greet you, Mother Cat, your father and my father, Toothless Tommy, when it's your time to cross over the bridge. Meow meoow!

Bernie: And we will all be there to greet you Grey, and Little One too, when it's your time to take the journey and cross the rainbow bridge.
You've been the best feline brother Grey, I'll always be watching over you.

Mr. Grey: I love you Bernie and I'm going to miss my Buddie and all our adventures. You've been the best Pal and brother any feline could ever have, but I still have Little One to take care of and our human Mom and Gary too. I'll see you again one of these days. I'm sure going to miss you. Meow Meoow.

Bernie: Meoooow.
Together they bunt heads and rub the length of each others sides. Tails up.

It turns out Bernie had an undefined type of carcinoma. It was aggressive and in a location anatomically that would make surgical removal very difficult if not impossible.

"Good Morning Bernie," I said in my morning voice. Instantly I felt Bernie's absence from his usual sleeping spot behind my bent knees. Typically he would wrap himself tightly against that spot keeping us both warm and feeling safe through the night. Other mornings he would be laying on his back in between us with his paws tucked under his chin and his tiny head on one of our pillows.

"I see you over there in the corner Bernie. Thank you for trying to sleep with us last night." Initially, when we first went to bed, he was with us. I heard him in the middle of the night having difficulty breathing and stirring quite a bit.

I reached out to him with my hand while still in bed wiggling my fingers for him to come to me, always one of his favorite games. With great effort he slowly staggered over to me and rubbed my hand with his cheek. He attempted to climb up on the bed but he couldn't. Instead, he stood on his back hunches and reached up to my hand with both his paws. His little paw pads felt warm on my fingers and the palms of my hands. "Bernie I'll come down to you." I crawled out of bed and sat on the floor next to him. He laid down on my lap. He purred but it was a struggle for him. He coughed and gagged. He tells me this isn't our usual morning routine and he prefers to do what's familiar to him at this hour of the day. So I stood up and he led the way to begin our customary habits. Although he's unable to watch me from his usual place next to the sink, he laid at my feet while I brushed my teeth and washed my face. Mr. Grey and Little One joined us as they always do this time of day, but on this day, both Mr. Grey and Little One guard Bernie. Little One went to Bernie first and gave him a long loving head bunt and a cheek rub. Mr. Grey watched with loving eyes sitting on the other side of him. With Bernie laying on my feet, and the other two laying on either side of him, I spoke softly to them and gave them each a little rub on the top of their heads and ears. Then down we all went to the kitchen to complete the remainder of our early morning activities. I made the coffee and while it was brewing placed their small individual bowls on the cat mat as they sat in their usual places waiting for what would come next. The ritual of Half and Half which they've come to expect since inside Mother Cats womb. After I poured a small amount into each of their bowls Mr. Grey began rapidly lapping it up as he had for years, knowing if he didn't, Bernie, who always would be finished with his portion first would bump Mr. Grey from his bowl and finish the rest of his. Always a double breakfast for Bernie. But on this morning Mr. Grey stopped lapping and just sat there staring at his small yellow bowl still full of half and half. Bernie tried, but he was unable to eat or drink. With his head hung low he walked away from our morning routine and went to his condo. He couldn't climb up. He let out a deep, low, loud howl. My heart began to ache, a piercing ache and my face felt flushed with heat. He slowly returned to the kitchen and walked towards Mr. Grey and Little One who were still sitting at their places staring at their bowls. He gave both of them head bunts and licked Little One at the top of her head in between her ears…then slowly staggering, he went back up stairs, where he retreated himself in a corner of the small yellow sunroom facing the west side of our house.

Butterflies surrounded me the following day.

I saw a shooting star tonight. It went from right to left, east to west. From where the sun rises to where the sun sets.

It's been years since I witnessed such brilliance in the sky and even longer for me when I last experienced the Perseids.

I was standing behind our home in front of our lavender garden. It was the week of the super moon in August 2014. It was a Tuesday evening and an experience that surely I will always remember, for its significance proved to be a sign to me, a sign that came from a loving heart.

8/5/2014

CONCLUSION

I have been writing this story since Mother Cat arrived all those years ago. I have spent countless hours creating poems and documenting their feline lives through short stories and journals. I was never motivated to finish the project, or perhaps, I just took for granted that all of their stories would continue indefinitely. On August 7, 2014 that changed. When you lose your pet, a member of your family, it's nothing short of heart wrenching. It's been only 11 days since our loss and Bernie's absence has been felt by each and every member of our family. Mr. Grey and Little One are figuring out their new social structure and Gary and I feel a tremendous void in the routines that we've come to expect. Our little Bernie crossed the Rainbow Bridge on August 7, 2014. Just two months shy from what would have been his eighth year anniversary of when he arrived on our doorsteps and just possibly, eight years from what would have officially been his eighth birthday. These feline stories will continue, but this story is in honor of all the joy, lessons and bountiful memories our feline pal Bernie gave to us, and to all those felines who have never been given a chance to find their own joyful families during their lifetime.

Butterflies for Bernie
Light from the super moon
This was on a Tuesday
His end was all too soon
Butterflies for Bernie
Light from the super moon
The stars are dancing for him
His entrance sings hearts tunes.
9/12/2014

Mr. Grey's Glossary of Terms

Alpha Cat ~ Head cat, big cheese, CEO, Director, the Cat in Charge.

Bunt (ing) ~ A cat hello. A friendly greeting communicated by bumping the top of each other's heads.

Cat Acceptance ~ Blinking eyes slowly.

Colony ~ A large outdoor cat family.

Donut Bed ~ A small cozy round fleece bed.

Growl ~ Keep your distance. I'm scared of you be scared of me.

Heavy Side Layer ~ Loomis himself could take credit for this discovery! One of several layers of the earth's ionosphere reflecting medium frequency radio-waves. T.S. Elliott first introduced this term in his book *Old Possum's Book of Practical Cats*. Refers to cat heaven.

Kitty Condo ~ A multi-level Complex with 360 degree views not subject to Tuxedo Park Architectural review board.

Mousing ~ Cats + Mice = 0 Mice. A fun game for kitties.

Neuter ~ Refers to the feline male. No more evening prowls. How to help kitty become an outstanding citizen and socially acceptable household cat.

Rainbow Bridge ~ An anonymous poem that describes what happens to pets in their new life when they leave planet earth.

Runt ~ The weakest and smallest member of a litter. My brother Bernie broke this feline myth too because eventually he grew to be the strongest and most athletic of us all.

Shimmey ~ A method of sliding or crawling down haunches first, on a tall height or object, as in a tree.

Spay ~ Female kitty will be free to just be and every Tom cat will flee.

Tail Up ~ A happy cat.

Tail Up Shaking ~ A really happy cat, "I like you a lot."

AUTHOR'S NOTE ON SOURCES

Grateful Acknowledgement is made to the following:

Ancestory.com, Alfred Lee Loomis Residence; United States Census: Tuxedo Park, New York 1920, 1930, 1940

Conant, Jennet *Personal Interview* Host Brian Lamb June 9 2002 Booknotes C_SPAN

Conant, Jennet *Tuxedo Park A Wall Street Tycoon and the Secret Palace of Science that Changed the Course of World War 11*: New York, New York: Simon & Schuster 2002

John Foreman, "Inside Paxhurst." *Bigoldhouses.blogspot.com*/2010/11/inside-paxhurst.html. John Forman. Nov. 13, 2010. Web. Sept. 6, 2013.

Winslow, Foster Albert *Tuxedo Park A Journal of Recollections:* Tuxedo Park, New York: The Tuxedo Historical Society 1992

20859606R00054

Made in the USA
San Bernardino, CA
26 April 2015